Mental Warfare

Joseph Graham

Presentation by *BookLeaf Publishing*

Web: www.bookleafpub.com

E-mail: info@bookleafpub.com

ISBN: 9789360949228

First edition 2024

Dedicated to my father (Tavares) and my grandfather (Jeffery). Hoping my words reach you guys as y'all rest. I love you.

Author Preface

I'm Almighty Luck and poetry is my therapy. I just hope my demons are not too much for y'all.......

As you dive deep into my past traumas and things I'm now starting to heal from, you'll be taken on an emotional rollercoaster. "It's okay not to be okay," is something I want you guys to hold on to as you continue to read. Also, that everyone has dark times and when life becomes too much, remember you always made it back to the light. You have strength within you even on the days you feel like giving up. There isn't a timetable for healing. Take your time and do it for you. Most of all, I'm thankful that you're still here.

Acknowledgment

I would like to thank everyone who believed in my vision and guided me on this journey. Everything from "I can't wait until your book is finished" to the people that had their own intimate touch in the progression of making Mental Warfare.

A special thanks to Ari. An extraordinary person and friend who brought my thoughts to life. From the cover to the different pieces throughout this book, her artistic touch was felt. I am grateful for the time and effort she put into this. Most importantly, the pride and excitement she had in creating each piece. I'm looking forward to the future work we do together.

Thank you to the different basketball coaches I had throughout my life. Teaching me discipline and accountability. Shout out to Coach P and Coach G for going further, teaching and speaking life into me. Helping me find a purpose outside of basketball.

Thank you to the world of poetry. Giving me a way to interact with life in ways that I didn't know were possible. To the people I've encountered in the community. Shout out to the Street Prophet who consistently motivated me to become a better poet, artist and most importantly a person. A special thanks to Shay for being my mentor and believing in me since the very beginning. She gave me the confidence to grow within myself which allowed me to start this journey.

Thank you to my family for shaping me into the person I am today. The good and the bad because without those experiences, I wouldn't be who I am. A special shout out to my mother, aunts and grandmothers for nurturing me and showering me with unconditional love. To my cousins and brother for motivating me to find my own path because being the youngest it was always hard to stand out. To my uncles, who taught me different ways to be a man in the absence of my father. A special thank you to my father and grandfather. Individually impacting my life at its foundation. Now, both are looking down on me, this will be my gift to them. Shout out to my cousin Jess for unintentionally giving me the title Mental Warfare in our group chat.

I am most of all thankful for the things I've been through. Molding me into the person I am today. I'm grateful for the growth and learning that I'm doing. I take pride in my healing.

Almighty Testimonies

Sharpened Insecurities

I emit so much confidence but deep down, I still
have so much shyness.
I want to lower my brightness, but attention
always finds me.
Maybe it's the Leo in me or being 6'4.
Carrying myself with so much poise...
It's the demeanor for me!
Unknown that I am fumbling over my words
when I am not even talking.
You would assume that my love language is
overthinking the way I'm obsessed with it.
My soulmate, the way it is entangled with my
spirit.
I'm here but not in reality.
I'm trapped on a mental plane where it gives me
dancing lessons.
Where my subconscious got to take control of
my representation because I have two left feet.
That is why I am always stumbling.
I have no balance within myself.
My polarity is off its fixture or is it the liquor?
The light...
The dark...
The mixtures.
I always need something stronger to escape the
depths of my mind.

It's like I'm surrounded by darkness.
Falling into Tartarus.
Where my doubt is a Titian, and my greatness is
Achilles.
I'm in a constant battle with an enemy that
knows my weakness.
Sharpening my insecurities, aiming straight at
my Achilles so I can't run from it.
Everytime I reach my peak radiancy, it drags me
back over like a Mortal Kombat fatality.
Get over here!
As it stands over my body.
Punching a hole where my heart is.
Slapping my will onto a sacrificial rock and it
feels like I'm losing everything!
It feels like...
I have no one to back me up because I sit at a
table all alone as red drips down...
As red drips down and I become a pile of dead
weight.
What did I do to deserve this weight?

Priceless

My energy is priceless but lately I have been
letting everyone punch in like Tyson!
Clueless that I was investing in source-less
entities.
Allowing deposits from insufficient funds when
I was giving out fortunes.
Extortion from the people I hold dear.
Depleting my shares for who would vanish when
I need little bit care.
I've been facing despair when no one is nearby.
I've grown accustomed to disappearing instead
of asking for help because for me, no one is truly
there.
A burden I came to bear but still lend a hand
when I hear someone else's cries.
Maybe it's how I was raised?
Receiving my mother's generous ways.
Or I'm just a people pleaser who doesn't know
how to say no.
The most loyal or the stupidest.
A stewardess in the art of pleasing but never
dismissing.
Maybe it's a mission from divinity.
Embedding a large amount of empathy.
A coping mechanism to avoid my own vacancy.

Steadily engulfing myself in everyone else's
misery.
Knowing that the energy I receive takes a toll on
me, but I continue to indulge in things that's no
good for me.
I'm the biggest danger to me than any weapon
formed against me!
Self-inflicted wounds that could have been
avoided.
Mental trauma that still needs to be sorted.
I just want to be dormant, but everybody keeps
calling and I keep enduring...

Truly Love Me?

My phone doesn't ring but everybody loves me.
Then ask me why I'm silent when my body
language speaks loudly.

If you loved me, you would see that my mind is
cloudy.
That my eyes forecast for rain but I'm forcing
delays.

That my energy is off its relay.
That my demons are having a field day.

I can't shake these dark feelings I'm having
these days.
but I except someone who loves me to detect.

To get that sometimes I must detach to reattach.
Isolate to medicate but no one understands that.

They want you to shine through your darkness.
Be a beacon of hope when you need some
prayers.

So, I just smile because they can't relate to the
hurting of my essence.
They constantly misuse my presence.

Saying I'm precious but only when I have
blessings.
Never when I'm looking for guidance.

Silent when my mind is in a riot.
Their appearance becomes slim like they're
working on a diet.

Time after time I've been deserted.
Escorted into loneliness after I showed
genuineness, but I'm used to it...

It's embedded in my veins to care for someone
blues but when mine hits the surface, everyone
becomes cautious like they're seeing red.

A phobia of who I am on the inside.
Rather use my healing soul to heal their own.

Then run away when it's my turn.
Maybe they don't truly love me but just the idea
of me.

Constant Conflict

Do you know how it feels when your head
conflicts with your heart?
Trying to give CPR to something that doesn't
have lungs.
It's like something grasping around your neck.
Causing your veins to start popping like a pill
addict.

Making your eyes fluster in panic.
Redness starts a hostile takeover.
Enslaving your pupils.
Your tears try to flee the war zone.

Leaving a trail of pain.
I guess that's where scars come from.
I collected a lot over the years like souvenirs
from the places that I once held dear.
I fear that who I am is more than something
people can bear.

I used to be proud to be who I was.
I wear it like a Purple Heart but it's like I always
get stripped of my rank.
Like I didn't have enough in the tank for people
to ride without hitting the brakes.
Like my love was putting them on stake.

They must have seen me as a pilgrim who
couldn't understand their sorcery.
That my burning desire to be with them wasn't
to harm but to flourish.
Like Daenerys emerging from the flames, giving
her claim to a kingdom.
This was all I wanted, to give them a throne but
it's like I got the curse of the Targaryen's.

Burning everything in my wake.
And it gets me ousted from the place I was
trying to build, and my foundation became
sediment for someone else to construct on.
That someone else became the architect of their
happiness.

As I sat on the sideline, cheering for their win
because that is all I ever wanted but I can't help
not wanting to be put back in the game.
I remember learning plays to generate success
while the ball was in my court, but previous
injuries made me seem unfit.

So, I was tossed from the game.
Forced into rehab while they inserted another
player into their rotation.

Watching them while they felt like they were in the finals, so I demanded a trade!
I came to understand that I would never be the star in their eyes.

So, I made up my mind that I could be that for someone else.
But every time I visit their arena, it feels like home.
So, I'm torn when we come face to face.
My mind knows one thing and my heart feels another.

They stay in conflict like New York and Boston.
A rivalry inside me that I hope can't be told through my eyes cause the eyes are a gateway to the soul.
And my soul is still infatuated with theirs, but I must try to bury that because I'm no longer what they treasured but it's like I'm a relic.

Not good enough to wear like jewelry but still placed on the shelf for viewing.
I must be amusing.
Just enjoyment for the moment.
Cause I'm golden but also eroded.

My surface is polished but what's underneath
isn't worth it.
Causing another conflict of interest.
Constant conflict.
Maybe I'm the conflict that's constant.

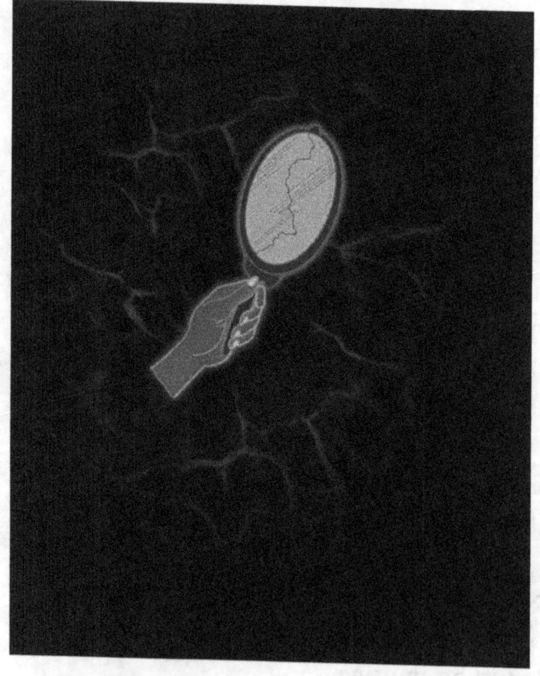

Rejection

Imagine having so much confidence that you
could overcome any situation.
Countless hours of building up your game to its
peak vibration.
Then you get the opportunity to showcase who
you are.
In your head, you're doing all the right things
but just like that, you get dismissed.
It's like a vacuum sucking the air out of you.
Your heart drops to what seems like a bottomless
pit.
In that moment, a picture is painted that you're
not good enough.
You see rejection comes in all shapes and sizes.
Unfortunately, I was a canvas of all its forms.
Illustrating my faults.
Hanging it on a wall where my soul fixates over
it.
Where my doubt becomes my highest bidder.
Placing me in a gallery where bitterness comes
and see it.
Hand in hand with those experiences like they're
on a date.
That image marinates.
Playing over and over.
Back-to-back.

It takes a shot for me to numb.
It works from time to time, but those moments
are too much.
Those dreams of Draft Day became the furthest
thing from me.
Reminiscing on all the sacrifices.
The fire and desire I had just to be told to go
home in the middle of tryouts.
It wasn't even about my skill; it was about my
conditioning.
Taking months off to take care of my financial
wellbeing.
Thinking that my passion fruit can survive
without watering.
Hoping my will could push me through, but I
wasn't in Bel-air.
I was in my feelings.
Being cut was supposed to fuel my redemption
but nothing was the same.
I lost my love for the game.
Or was it the fear of failing again?
Honestly, I was angry!
I put so much into this game.
Pouring my blood, sweat and tears just for what
I worked so hard for to be defamed.
Watching what I wanted so badly passed me by.
Hand in hand with bitterness, finishing their
date.
All I wanted was to curse it out.

Saying I didn't want you anyway but that was
just my pride being hurt.
Y'all know how men get when their ego has
been bruised.
Covering it with words of hatred.
Forsaken everything after.
A toxic healing practice to avoid shame but all I
feel is shame.

See Through

I had hoop dreams.
I was supposed to be the next big thing.
It was all in my genes, but it wasn't for me.
I lost myself in the vision of other people.
They only saw me as a player under the whistle.
Never saw my true potential.
It was disguised behind a person with similar
visuals.
A parent that's no longer visible so I'm chosen
to play out his what if scenarios.
I embraced it but the burden is unbearable.
I can never be the original!
Trying to separate my identity when we're
identical is a task so stressful.
Got me questioning who I am.
Not on the surface but underneath the layers.
The layers that's created by family delegators.
Who's oblivious to the fact that I have my own
purpose.
Every time I try to be my own sculptor, they
erode it.
Corroding my individuality.
Causing me to push my inner self deeper within
to satisfy everyone else's reality.
Forcing me to keep up an image that doesn't
picture me.
Got me falling victim to conformity.

Where my mind catches a battery against my
thoughts of singularity.
It would rather be stuck in confines when I want
to walk the path of Zuko.
Ever since those blue masks, I've been facing
twin swords.

Who they want me to be and who I am.
Causing a split in my mental accords.
I just want my own staff of Moses so I can split
these ongoing waves so I can keep moving
forward.

Towards my own relevance!
Towards my own anything!
I'm tired of walking in the shadow of a ghost.
I just want to be my own soul.
So y'all can see me and not through me.

Fatherless

You set the stage then vacated but your shadow
still eclipses me.
Your path or mine, those lines are blurred.
I want to walk in your footsteps but who am I
personally?
I took my mind out my body and thought how
come we never spoke but I'm always talking to
you?
I don't cry but I'm always shedding tears for you.
I started balling so I could be closer to you.
Looking to the stands, hoping you'll be there,
but every time your seat is empty.
Deep down, I'm empty!
Supposed to be here but shots rang out and left
your bloody body laid out.
We know how the story goes from here on out.
Another fatherless black child.
Another statistic in the system to be defiled.
So much anger being stockpiled but dress it up
with a smile.
I can't show the demons that need to be
reconciled.
I put so much into this style that my emotions
are exiled.
Now they're asking why I'm so distant.
I lost your existence before I knew of your
presence.

Put in a hearse before I learned how to mourn.
I'm still so torn.
I wish you weren't gone.
I wish you had that thing on you!
I rather than some holes in you.
Now I walk with a hole in me.
This emptiness is controlling me.
Why did you have to abandon me?
I know you didn't want this to be, but it still took
a toll on me.
Why can't the afterlife have a free way?
I'll visit you every day.
Ask you why you didn't go away.
You could have been balling, playing overseas.
I understand you wanted to take care of your
seed.
That was admirable but I just wish you weren't
tangible.
I wouldn't be so damaged.
Branded as fatherless.
They say time heals but it only makes things
worse.
That pain nurtures and grows.
So, you find ways to mend your lows but that
does more damage than healing.
I'm sick of it!
I'm tired of not feeling okay!
What must I do to take this pain away?

AA

Hi! I'm Joseph and I'm an alcoholic.
I've been told that I always have a bottle like a
genie.
Honestly, it's the only thing that helps me escape
like Houdini.
Giving me life lessons like Mr. Feeny because
I'm still a boy trying to meet this world.
This cruel, cruel world.
It's like pain is on a tour from my head to my
core and I haven't even healed from my first
loss.
That's probably why I'm still so lost.
The only time I find myself is when I am sauced.
When I'm under the influence, retcons occur,
causing changes to my lore.
Pre-Games become my origin story.
Whether it's light or dark determines my
personality.
Superman or Batman.
A billionaire playboy or a lover boy.
And most of the time, I mix the two so y'all can
get the best of both worlds.
When I'm trying to escape my own.
I would rather live in a dream state.

Infinite Tsukuyomi!

It's like I'm Sasuke and this liquor is Naruto.
Always trying to bring me back from the
darkness but I strive in the darkness!
When my back is against the wall, I find a way
to bring the thing that took everything from me
to its knees.

Even if it takes everything out of me and I pass
out from exhaustion but y'all would never see it
as that.

Y'all only see it as the gloss in my eyes and
think that I'm falling victim to this intoxication.
Effectuated with the wrong problems when I'm
stuck on a whole other equation.
Bringing up angles that have nothing to do with
the thing helps me function.
That what's in this cup, has the formula to my
survival but I'm forced to come to these
meetings and break myself down into factions.
Putting how I cope into parentheses. Pushing it
to the side.
It adds to my sobriety but multiplies my anxiety.
Dividing the thing that keeps me active socially.
Eventually, I subtracted myself from society.
Forcing me to find the power to stand on my
own without a crutch.
Y'all can put to the test but I still may fail
because math is complicated just like the human
mind.
And mine confuses loyalty with codependency.
Creating unhealthy relationships that I can't let
go of because the stain of withdrawal is more
than what I deposited.
Trapping me in a safe where I don't even feel
safe.

Slaves Anymore?

When I'm at my highest, you bring me to my
lowest.
Falling to pieces.
Thoughts in shambles.
Inside of me uneasy.
Please take it easy.
You've been a part of me for so long but do me
so wrong.
You're so toxic and don't even try to hide it.
Proud to belittle me ever since I was little.
I want to hide within me but I'm so silly, that's
where you always meet me.
You're so needy.
Becoming more and more greedy.
Appearing when I make an appearance.
Crowd full of people and I see you glaring.
You're waiting for my emotions to start flaring.
I wish we could start sparing.
I'm tired of this feeling!
I'm tired of being the odd one who shuts down
when everyone is talking.
I have so much to say but you're staying
repressed.
I'm tired of the missed opportunities!
All the time I couldn't embrace my greatness
because you had me feeling less.

I'm tired of the thought of cutting my own skin
to rip you from my flesh!
You're the cause of so much stress.
Why did you invest in me?
Laying the foundation for my vulnerability.
Amplifying my insecurities.
Slowly dismantling my sanity.
Blatantly impeding my growth so I can't be who
I want to be.
Anxiety! Enlighten me.
Why can't I be free?
I thought we weren't slaves anymore!

Sleepless Droughts

When the sun clocks out and blackness covers
the streets, is when I toss and turn in my sheets.
Not avoiding sleep but just can't fall asleep.
I tried counting sheep, but they didn't comfort
me.
That got to be a myth that doesn't account for
the darkness that comes to flirt with me.
Creeping in from the closet where the monsters
lurk.
Their shadows seeping into my dreams, making
them burst.
It's like I'm sinking, becoming drenched in my
own sweat.
This stress takes center stage.
Putting on the show for the ages.
Taking a bow for my devastation.
Shooting me down with no hesitation.
Giving me it's PTSD.
Post Traumatic Sleep Disorder!
I mean, Post traumatic stress!
I mean, I just want some rest, but it feels like
everytime
I close my eyes; it's like I'm cursed.
Nightmares tattooed on the inside of my eyelids!

I could never have them close; they always have
a counter bid.
Causing my thoughts and tiredness to try to
outbid one and other like my body is on auction.
I wish I had an option to do away with sleep.
Maybe it will be better for me.
I'm more productive when I'm awake but you
do need sleep to rejuvenate.
Being deprived of a natural reset will suffocate
your mental state but why am I always gasping
for air while I wake up abruptly?
Like 3 or 4 times a night.
I don't remember the last time I had a good
night's sleep.
Maybe before my demons realize that sleep is
my only sanctuary.
So, they brought out the cavalry to infiltrate my
dream state.
Making my psyche a war zone and I become the
only casualty.
Wishing I could scream but they drain me out
like a battery.

Plastering my tears on the wall like an art
gallery.
With such mastery.
All this agony because everything in my head is
crippling me.
I can't stand it!
So, I lean on Duse and Hennessy as a sedative.
Those blackouts are the only time the lights stay
out until the lights come back out.
I need another alternative to these sleepless
droughts.

Exhausted

I'm tired!
Not physically or mentally.
It's my soul.
It feels like it ran its course.
I've been looking for a source to replenish but
they always take advantage.
Adding on to what made me damaged like I was
an object in a demolition.
Breaking me down into lesser pieces like they
wanted to see me on cellular level but declined
when I needed answers.
Causing my battery to run low and the only
thing that feels right is being dead!
I no longer want to be plugged in.
You can take my eyes out of the socket because I
no longer see a reason to live.

This is my 13th reason why.
Life has always been putting me down.
No wonder I've become Tyler, ready to spray the
institute of my sorrows.
It's like we are born, and life becomes our rivals.
Liable to put us through hell just to see the light
at the end of the tunnel.
Never knowing how much of the darkness
consumes us.
Ever since our first breaths we've been fighting
to survive.
Survival of fittest.
This is the law of nature and God.
Giving his hardest battles to his strongest
soldiers but I didn't choose to be enlisted.
I didn't even choose to be here.
I thought we had free will.
So, I will dismiss these expectations!
These limitations shackled me to this existence.
I just want to be free to keep up my appearance.
I'm tired of putting on a brave face!
I'm tired of handling everything with grace!
I'm tired of running life's pace when it feels like
I'm stuck in place!
I am tired of hearing these sirens.
Trying to police these thoughts that have me lost
in this cave with no torch.
And it feels like these walls are caving in!

And it feels like I'm being emancipated from
this land because my will to live is leaking out
of my mind!
Assassinating my ability to withstand the hands
of death.
They wrap me in their arms, smothering the life
out of me as we lay in this presidential suite.
After years of battle with the darkest parts of my
estate.
There wasn't any union to stop the warfare and
the losses became too much.
Taking a toll on my spirit and I don't have
frequent flier miles.
It's like I'm climbing Mount Everest every time I
get out of bed.
The air becomes too thin, and I feel chills like
ghosts are visiting.
Maybe they can tell me how my soul gets some
rest because it's exhausted.

Plot Twist

I'm okay is a role I play in this movie called life.
I am known as one the greatest actors to touch
the silver screen.
Winning Oscars for my performances.
They sit on my shelf, reflecting on the life I
dream of but who am I behind the scripts?
If I'm stripped of the character that I developed,
would y'all see my plot twist?
Or will y'all still be blind to the conflict?
That I'm the antagonist of my own story.
That I've been wanting to slit my wrist just to get
a glimpse of what y'all see in me.
But all I see in me is a white flag-stained red.
Ironic, all my films have been about not giving
up.
Rising above the hardship.
Fight until you can't fight anymore.
Even if you can't move your body, your
thoughts are still your most powerful weapon
but what if it falls into the hands of the enemy?
The inner me!
Who's not even a fan of mine.
Rather see me do suicide in a scene.
So, my eulogy can break the box office.
Cause who would have known a star would have
put himself in a box.

But do y'all now see the plot twist or am I still
stuck in my role like Hugh Jackman?
Trying to claw my way from being the greatest
showman to being a real person that's on his last
stand!
Who's been drowning but y'all only see him
smiling and hear his laughter's like he's not
another Robin Williams…
Hanging on by a thread but there's no needle to
stitch him back together.
The fabric of his existence is unraveling but he
continues to put on great performance after great
performance because he's mastered at putting on
shows.

So, I guess y'all will only understand the plot twist when my character abruptly comes to an end like Chadwick, and I put on this black suit with my arms crossed.
I just hope y'all can remember me forever.

Lost The Joy

I lost joy but still have love for it.
I should have let it go but it got me frozen in
place.
Trapped in its gaze, it's the only thing that stops
me from unraveling at the seams.
Stitching my thoughts and feelings together like
they're at a broidery.
It's camaraderie between things that normally
can't coexist together.
It's an endeavor that leaves me in a burning rage
as I use all my might to be one for all.
Not the fragment that stains my conviction to
being worthy.
I'm thirsty to be great but I fear I have no depth
to channel my inner reservoirs.
I've been drowning in my failures.
Causing me to be submerged under my fears.
Psychological warfare that impairs my vision
like I don't have Hawkeyes.
Like my right hand isn't Black Widow that inks
poison.
That's probably why every time I fall, it feels
like death.
Where's the gem in that?
We're supposed to learn from our misfortunes,
but they hold me hostage.

With no ransom.
So, I'm stuck in bondage like I'm into BDSM.
When my kink is supposed to be dominance!
Making this stage submit to me and there's no safe word because I'm pounding it until it screams my name.
Reminding it that I beat it up the best.
Making it climax but this isn't the ending.
I can go on for rounds.
Finding its sweet spots but the way I intercourse is aggressive.
It sends a message that I can keep up with any drive.
That's why I got to take off the boot that keeps me parked.
You see my mind is a lot.
I went through every level to fight for my spot.
Forgetting that this is supposed to be my art.
Not something that takes me apart.
Breaking me down like I'm a product.
Trying to find the difference in what makes my pen high.
When I just want to handle the influence of my emotions.
Reroute my trauma but y'all applauded me.
Telling me y'all expect more for me when I feel less of me.
Teaching me the lesson that I must pour out my heart just to receive a Purple Heart.

When I just wanted to express what makes my
heart dark.
The filters I must go through just to bring
awareness to what makes me ill.
My mind took a spill and it's no pill to heal.
So, I just got to kill Bill just to see the joy on
y'all faces because I don't experience it
anymore.
I just feel like I must prove myself in something
I love.
Like why is being in love so draining?
Is what we have unhealthy?
I thought we communicated well but it's like we
don't comprehend each other.
I feel like we must take a break or even start
over.
Cause I don't want to lose what we have but it is
not supposed to feel like this.
So, if space is needed, I'll give you the moon so
we can eventually eclipse what brought us light
once again.

Writer's Block

Call the suicide hotline.
There's no longer a filter for my trauma.
Its toxins baptized me, and my angel abandoned me.
Forsaken me!
Knowing it's my only salvation.
Freeing me from the chains of my mind.
My head is a torturing room.
Sawing off parts of my soul.
Jig sawing my will to live.
With one wrong thought that sent me to purgatory, but this pen reached down for the heavens and saved me.
Having a bigger impact on my life than any higher power.
So, what am I supposed to do when I can't
Fucking!!!
I know that death has been waiting.
It's ready to nail me to a cross.
Watch the light leak out of me.
Bathe me in the darkness like all the times I break down in the shower.
In silence because no one understands me.
I have been trying to be open, but I stay getting triggered.
Causing me to jam up.

Searching for a new clip but they're always empty.
That's probably why I keep coming up blank.
I got to get away from this block like I'm done with the streets!
It's not safe for me.
I don't even feel relief when I slide home.
I stay boxing with my four walls.
Those diameters are killing me.
Trig was something I was never good at.
That's probably why I don't understand my triggers.
They create angles just to function with me, but I can never compute.
Making me feel obsolete.
So, I mix formulas just so I can feel complete but that only puts me in another dimension.
On a tangent with my demons.
Co-sign to the thoughts of taking my own life.
So, when I say I can't **FUCKING!!!**

I'm on the opposite side of the light.
Adjacent to the hands of death.
That's just to prepare for the SAT.
The Sacrifice of Almighty Testimonies.
In holy matrimony with the reaper.
He's just waiting for my feature.
Signing me to a 360 but I can't produce.
I'm in breach of my contract.

My rights are owed to him.
That's probably why when I CAN'T FUCKING
WRITE,
IT IS DEATH!!!

Death Note

I don't believe in my pen anymore.
That it could be my salvation.
Realizing that its divinity was just an illusion.
Brainwashing me to believe in it like Manson.

Portraying that I'm doing all these killing when
it's behind the body bags.
I've been zipped tied to the stories it has created
so y'all won't see the person behind the words.
That who y'all see is a false identity.
Masquerading as the brave and the bold when
I'm still reliving my darkest knights!

I've been masking my pain and that has been
robbing me of my truth.
I'm not as strong as I claim to be.
I'm only here because I was too weak to go
through with it.
The sermons that I wrote are not testimonies,
they are my failures to commit.

That's probably why I have a problem with love.
Exchanging a pen for a person but they still
serve the same purpose.
Something to hold but not to handle well.

Making me lose my grip on what's important to
me because all the bull I went through has
blinded me to the point where I can't feel.

There's no Braille for being numb.
So, what are you supposed to do when you lose
your only way to see through the pain?
You use your other senses but you're only able
to tap in with your 6th.
Seeing dead people with the same unresolved
issues.

These suicidal thoughts.
That breaks you down into sections.
Making me hand off parts of myself to strangers.
Receiving pounds of recognition but no one ever
sees that my goodwill was an act!

Hunting for places for my poems to save
someone else's life.
When my life is on its way out.
People always have ulterior motives and mine
was for my pen to lead me to the afterlife.
While leaving behind scriptures to uplift others.

For my words to be carved into my tombstones.
Hoping that I was good enough for people to
come visit me after my last performance.
To give me my flowers!

Maybe I could finally understand how much I
meant to others.

That I didn't need to hide behind this pen.
I'm trying to find courage in it.
Claiming that I got that dog in me when all I'm
feeling is pink.
Sick of my paranoia.

Tired of battling the monster of my mind.
There wasn't no Muriel to show me love.
Only that nigga Eustace, who makes me feel
useless.
Just like this pen.

I've been puppeteered by it.
Having it exploits the darkest part of soul.
Giving a home to thoughts of taking my own
life.
So, was this pen ever my savior?

Or was it just a scythe….
To my death note?

Untitled

A couple days ago my niece looked at me.
Her face filled with so much concern and she
walked over to hug me.
She then asked me, why did I look sad?
At that moment I wanted to break down, but I
couldn't allow my tears to fall in front of her.
She's too precious to witness my cries that are
filled with so much pain.
In her arms, her heartbeat pulsed louder the
noises in my head.
My life began to flash before my eyes for the
times I thought about leaving this earth.
Thinking about how I could leave her, but she
held me tighter, and I felt her love breathing life
back into me.
When she let me go, my first instinct was to
reassure her that I was okay, and I realized that I
was a pathological liar.
Wired to deny how I feel especially to the people
who care for me.
To hide that I'm broken and need help.
So, I won't be seen as ill but I'm sick and tired.
I'm sick and tired!
I am sick and tired of being here!
Being cuffed to the walls of anxiety.
Bound to the floors of insecurities.

Behind the bars of feeling alone with guards that drag their batons across those said bars.
Echoing the sounds of emptiness through the box that I've been thrown in.
As I live out the sentence of me being alive, I sit solitary.
Where the darkness is my only visitor.
It whispers, *why do you keep putting yourself through this when it hurts you.*
Do you not love yourself enough to let go?
How many times are you going to let your mind go to pieces in search of mental peace when you could just sleep?
The pain will go away....

Art Not My Eulogy

I'm depressed.
Yes, I have a therapist and this stage is very
therapeutic.
So, I come up here, in a room full of people I
don't know because I realized that y'all will only
see what I go through as art and not my eulogy.
Receiving me in my purest form.
Allowing my negativity essence, expression
without undermining how I feel.
Y'all listen to me rather than talking over me.
Trying to get answers out of me when I don't
even know what's going on within me.
That I'm a foreigner within my own body!
I have been having these intrusive thoughts that
colonized the entirety of my being.
Enslaving my wellbeing!
Putting me on a stage with my arms bound to
pillars.
You would've thought this was a crucifixion, but
I didn't die for anyone's sins.
I died from the cost of living!
No religion gave me enough faith for me to
believe I can be saved.
So, death has been engraved into my palms.
My lifeline is coming to completion because my
life has not been feeling complete.

I'm always trying to make the end meet but it's
like its inflation on being alive.
There's no financial aid for death.
It always comes to collect.
Whether you do it yourself or it is garnish.
It's astonishing how clever I can say I want to
die and expect that someone can read between
the lines.
Knowing the way, I illustrate my darkness on the
canvas of y'all ears, it will only be heard as
gospel and not a cry out for help.
I try to generate tears so y'all can see my pain
but it's like my inner reservoirs are empty.
My inner self is empty.
No wonder I stay trying to get something from
strangers.
My soul is homeless.
Looking for change but there is always an empty
can, but I'm done recycling my breaths.
It's like I'm always fighting for my life but
lately, I've been getting my ass whooped.
Putting me on my deathbed and this poem are
my last words.
I signed up for DNR because I don't want to be
brought back once I finally flatline because I lost
my will to live.

Cry Out for Help

My psyche is a war zone and I've been wanting
to wave the white flag.
I just need to silence the noise.
It's like screeching on the inside of my mind.
Carving out what makes me whole, and I evolve
into a walking corpse.
It's like I'm here but not living.
So hollow but it's no G to stop my demons from
going off the deep end. Me and my demons
become besties.
Maybe even lovers.
Our favorite position became missionary.
It stares into my eyes but there's no soul behind
those gateways.
As I release into them, they lock their legs
around my empty body.
Trapping what's left of me within them, while I
fall asleep while I'm still inside.
And that's what you call soul ties.
They whisper in my ear like *"you already came
for me; you matter well come home with me
where the flames are the brightest
Our spark can become a supernova.
A precursor to the death of a star.
You will no longer have to escape the black
holes that try to consume you."*

As I slept, their words caressed my deepest,
darkest desires that I try not to let inspire.
Giving a home to thoughts that's supposed to be
outliers.
Igniting a fire that's so memorizing that I get lost
in its flickers like Lil Wayne's lighter.
The heat that it gives off slowly engulfs me.
And I evolve once again, to something I truly
fear but that's the only time the noises cease to
exist.
When I'm thinking of not existing.
Weighing if my existence even matters.
Like if I'm gone in an instant, would anyone
realize that it wasn't instant?
That I have been drowning and that's what made
me distant.
That my okays have way more substance.
That okay is the universal signal to give
assistance even when there's resistance!
Or are we too ignorant or too arrogant to believe
that one can take our own existence?
Like "not my baby" when your baby has been in
a stillborn state ever since life has been a
miscarriage.
They have been dead on the inside, and you
have just been a necrophiliac.
Giving them love but the type of love they need
is something you lack.

So naive to what they need to be brought back
because you never listen to their okays.
Their okay was a cry for help, but you were deaf
and that was what truly killed them.
Not having no one to understand them.
Or anyone to talk to about how they're losing
their will to live.
How are we supposed to know what to do when
our thoughts become too crippling?
Shattering your psyche.
Triggering an ongoing war and the losses
becomes too much.
And the only thing that feels right is giving up.
You tried all the highs.
Even drank every bottle to the bottom but the
intoxication has no sensation.
You're craving relations to save you, but the
demons are the only thing that brought you
stimulation.
So, to my demons, you have won.
I will get on one knee and give you the thing
that's supposed to be in my chest.
So, I can finally put these noises to rest.
Thank you for always being here when I had no
one else.

Alone

Ever felt like a needle in a haystack?
Surrounded by so many but can't relate to any.
Like we're family but through marriage.
Connected but no strings attached.
So detached like Stefan when he turns off his
emotional latch.
Becoming the ripper to my own dairies.
I cut the throats of my relationships because I
lost the signal to broadcast communications.
Now encased in isolation because it's the only
comfortable situation.
Being by myself gives me a sensation.
I never felt safe in a congregation.
They send around a collection that leaves me to
question their intentions.
Saying they love me but never took the time to
get to know me.
I must be a character on a T.V. Show.
Y'all don't know the person behind what I'm
portraying.
Picturing me one way but I have multiple angles
like an octagon.
I've been fighting the urge to be withdrawn but
every time I allow deposits, they are insufficient
and bounce back.

I've gotten used to these transactions, so they are
the only ones I expect from people that bank
with me.
They eventually always close with me, and I'm
left with their debt.
Bankrupting other people's access to me.
I no longer trust the business of others.
Nor do I think they understand my contractual
agreement.
I don't even get it myself.
I have been trying to decode my own content but
it's like a Rubik's cube.
Interlocking in many ways.
So, I'm never present, just stuck in my mind.
Especially in a room full of people that don't get
me.
I don't even understand myself.
It's like there's a doppelgänger in my body that
traps me in the sunken place.
For me to gain control of us, I must go to war
with myself.
At the end, there's always someone that gets
buried and once again, I'm all alone.
So how can y'all expect anything more when
inside myself, I'm so lonely?

How Do You Deal with Death?

How do you deal with death when it feels like
you're dying?
Their last moments replaying like it was the
number one highlight on sports center.
It is being broken down by the voices in your
head.
Telling you what you should have done.
What you could have done but everyone on the
outside saying you did all that you can.
That I can't think about it.
Shake it out of your head.
Not knowing it is engraved on your spirit.
That my grandmother's cries scream at my soul.
And the image of us dragging his lifeless body.
His legs buckling,
fills my stomach like an unwanted fetus.
I need to get rid of it, but we know how Roe v
Wade went.
Then being told to give him CPR with no
knowledge of CPR.
Not knowing if I'm doing the right or wrong
thing.
The EMTS came in periodically or was it even
periodically?

I was pressing my hands against his chest like I
was trying to understand the definition of
insanity as I waited for EMTs to finally step in.
I stepped into my thoughts as they had the same
results as me, like we copied each other's
answers on a test but we both failed.
I guess we weren't scholars.
So, they rushed him to the hospital to people that
supposedly had honors.
Separating me and my grandmother when she
needed me the most.
Bending the air out me as I hear her agony when
she calls me from the hospital.
Telling me to
"Hurry up!
My husband is dead, and they won't let me see
him."
I don't think anyone would ever understand
what that did to me.
So, I'll ask y'all again, how do you deal with
death when it feels like you're dying?

Dear Dad,

As blood leaked out of you, something in me
drained out simultaneously.
Altering the way, I deal with things
fundamentally.
Causing me to push away my feelings so I won't
feel the same loss that you gave me.
But somehow, I still fall victim to letting
someone in.
They jump into my pool of emptiness.
Filling it up until they can't handle the depths.
Evacuating the premises when I started to
drown.
Causing me to latch on.
Never knowing to let go because I thought they
were my lifeguards.
Their existence administering CPR.
Breathing dependency into my lungs.
Becoming so attached like an IV bag.
I drained myself into them by the tons.
Passing out because I gave up too much.
Trying to fill the void that you left.
It always comes back to how you left.
Why couldn't you fight to come back?
People come back from the worst.
I know this isn't fair, but I have an unquenchable
thirst for us to be close.

I have been trying to bridge the gap like
Hiemdall.
Even started living out your dream through me,
but it created a dark hold over my heart.
I've grinded my soul to mimic the vision of you,
but it still wasn't enough.
I still couldn't fill what was missing.
I wish I could feel the chills from you visiting
but it's like you're always ghosting.
I am always writing to you, but you stay, leaving
me on read.
I just wish I could be seen by you!
For you to acknowledge me but it's like I'm
never on your agenda.
Do I need to become an Avenger?
Gather the stone to snap you back into reality
because my reality has been nothing but what
ifs.
What if you didn't leave the crib?
What if something jammed his grip?
What if you had that thing on you to make his
blood drip?
I would rather have that than him putting you in
a bag that needed to be zipped.
I am pissed that I was too young to spin back!
Even though he was put in a pack, the feeling of
me standing over his body, giving him a head
tap can't be matched.
I am pissed that time doesn't heal.

I can't swallow the pill that your faith has been
sealed.
I wish I could burn the field of reeds because
how can you have eternal peace when I don't
have internal peace?
I'm still grieving while you sleep in peace but
are you even at peace knowing you left your
seeds with something that impedes what they
need to exceed?
I'm pissed that I'm so pissed!
I just wish the afterlife had a mailing list.
Maybe it could fill this rift that makes me lose
my grip on reality.
My sanity is based on your vacancy.
That's probably why my soul stays in solitary.
Solitude confines me and it's all because I can't
confide in you.
I've been searching for clues to escape these
blues.
This notepad is the only thing that's stopping me
from being next to you and if that's the only
thing that's stopping me from being with you, I
finally know what to do.
I know you probably just want me to live for
you but lately, I haven't been feeling alive.
So, what am I supposed to do?
I just hope whatever I do you can approve.

Love, your son.

Love Myself

I love myself but I only say it when I'm reading
this poem.
Nor do I believe it.

For a long time, I didn't know anything about
affirmation or self-love.
That these words are powerful, and I was
gullible.

Believing anything people say to me when they
don't even know me.
But damn, do I even know myself?

I never took the time to sit down and talk with
me.
My inner voice, not even me.

It's the tone of my dead father that I never even
heard.
A coping mechanism that I still don't
understand.

That's probably why I have a problem with
loving myself.
There's tension between my trauma and who I
am.

Causing overwhelming, conflicting thoughts.
That makes me feel so lost.

In search of a torch in other people's thoughts.
With smoke that's hazardous.
Cancerous to my wellbeing.

Chemo is my silence and being at a distance.
Going further away from reality.

Cause I'm just a casualty.
A victim of verbal warfare.

Wearing war wounds as my personal attire.
Matching my pre-existing flaws.

Giving me PTSD when my skin started to
discolor like Jackson.
Joe has been beating my self-esteem ever since I
was learning my ABCs.

I always hated the man in the mirror.
It was D-Day reflecting on me, but I never
received a medal of honor.

Just a prosthetic where my heart used to be.
Tin man from the Wiz would have loved this.

So how could I be so brainless but courageous in
the thoughts of not being here?
The dead lean on me but I want to tell them to
beat it.

To prove that this death wish doesn't rock my
world.
So, I can finally say,

The love I have for myself never felt so good
and can't get enough.
I learned that my healing isn't black and white.
It will go to different pigmentation as I try to
escape the box my trauma places me in.

As it highlights my insecurities with every step I
take. No Billie Jean but I'm the one who
moonwalks through all my bad.

Giving myself an experience of a lifetime. So
from here on out, I'm telling heaven it can wait
because
I'm now learning how to say I love myself and
actually mean it.